William Graham Sumner, Abraham L. Earle

Our Revenue System and the Civil Service

Shall they Be Reformed?

William Graham Sumner, Abraham L. Earle

Our Revenue System and the Civil Service
Shall they Be Reformed?

ISBN/EAN: 9783337296087

Printed in Europe, USA, Canada, Australia, Japan

Cover: Foto ©Suzi / pixelio.de

More available books at **www.hansebooks.com**

OUR REVENUE SYSTEM

AND

THE CIVIL SERVICE.

SHALL THEY BE REFORMED?

BY

ABRAHAM L. EARLE.

NEW YORK:
PUBLISHED FOR
THE NEW YORK FREE TRADE CLUB,
BY
G. P. PUTNAM'S SONS,
182 FIFTH AVE.
1878.

NOTE.

THE first edition of this pamphlet was issued in
1871. Since then five editions have been published.
With some revisions, and with a few pages addition
to the matter, the seventh year of its existence is em-
phasized by the publication of the seventh thousand,
together with an introductory by Prof. W. G. Sumner.

March, 1878.

INTRODUCTORY.

THE Tariff System has long been an impediment to our National prosperity, and a most fruitful source of sectional strife. It has been perverted from the purpose for which it was adopted—to furnish revenue; and has become a most corrupt and formidable obstacle to the pursuit of useful and honorable enterprise.

The Custom House and Internal Revenue System is rapidly increasing and concentrating patronage and power under the control of the Federal Government. These are already gigantic in proportions, corrupt in character, and most dangerous to our liberties. To wield this patronage and this power is, more than all things besides, the stimulus for party supremacy, but it is the very element which no party can safely be trusted to control.

The Federal Constitution provides for Direct Taxation by apportionment of Government expenses among the several States according to population and representation. Taxes so apportioned may be collected through the agency of the respective States by whatever method they may severally prefer. In this way the services of thousands of federal office-holders will be dispensed with, thus effecting a complete reform in these departments and preparing the way for thorough purification in other departments of Government.

(3)

PREFACE.

IT seems to me that the foolishest thing free-traders can now do is to fall to quarreling with each other about how much free trade they want. For my part I want all the free trade I can get. I am not afraid of too much. The case is such that any and all who want tariff reform can join and push on with all the strength they can muster. They will not get any more than the most timid one wants, until he has had full time to reflect, and to withdraw if he wants to. If any one will join I do not see the propriety of warning him not to fight too hard, or not to believe in the cause too much. The methods of a popular agitation are not those of an academical discussion. The allies who can be most profitably dispensed with, in a popular discussion, are those who only get in the way.

I have consented to write a preface to this book, not because I want to help to propagate the positive views contained in it; I leave them to stand on their own merits. If I were to criticise them, I should have to write another book. It may suffice to say that I hold the experience of the United States, in their internal relations, to be a complete demonstration that the best arrangement of trade and industry for the

i

whole world would be absolute freedom of exchange,
each State providing by internal taxation for the support of law, order, security, and civil institutions
within its own borders. All taxes on commodities are
taxes on labor. The notion of taxing luxuries only,
or chiefly, is illusory. If taxes fell only on the luxuries of the rich they would produce little revenue.
"Luxury" is a term without a definition. Such
terms always produce confusion in thought. The
articles which produced the largest revenue in 1877
were the following:

	Consumption.	Average duty on dutiable.	Revenue.	Consumption per capita.*	Duty per capita.
Silk and mfs. of.........	$28,400,000	58.85 per cent.	$12,800,000	61.22 cts.	27.46 cts.
Sugar........	1,486,000,000 lbs. $71,800,000	2.36 cts. per lb., equal to 47.7 per ct. ad valorem	$34,300,000	31.87 lbs. $1.54	73.65 cts.
Wool and mfs. of....	$33,400,000	60.53 per cent.	$20,200,000	71.77 cts.	43.45 cts.

* Population estimated by the Bureau of Statistics, 46,600,000.

These three articles produced, in a year of great
depression, $67,300,000, or more than half the total
customs revenue. They are all heavily protective, and
cost the people in contributions to "home producers"
more than the other half of the revenue. The figures
show that these articles, if luxuries at all, are luxuries
of the poor in this country. The first luxury towards
which "the poor" reach out, when their circumstances
rise, is food and drink, and the next is female ap-
parel. Tea and coffee bore no revenue.

	Consumption.	Do. per capita.	Revenue per capita.
Coffee.....	332,000,000 lbs. $53,600,000	7.12 lbs. $1.15	3 cts. per lb. would yield $9,900,000 or 21.36 cts.
Tea........	58,900,000 lbs. $16,000,000	1.26 lbs. 34.3 cts.	15 cts. per lb. would yield $8,800,000 or 18.9 cts.

Spirits, wines, and beer produced $5,900,000, or 12.77 cts. per head; tobacco produced $4,300,000 or 9.22 cts. per head. These latter articles were under a heavy excise tax, so that they were not protected, or but little protected, and the consumption of home commodities produced revenue.

EXCISE.

Revenue.	Per capita.
Spirits............$57,400,000.........	$1.23
Tobacco........... 41,100,000.........	.88
Fermented Liquors.. 9,400,000.........	.20

107,900,000

Out of a total of....118,900,000

Thus we have a large consumption of articles of food and drink, and of tobacco, per capita, and although it has declined somewhat during the hard times, the figures show that the vast mass of the people are suffering no "distress." After these "luxuries" come the luxuries of dress, represented under silk and wool, for by far the heaviest items under this latter head are women's dress goods (consumption $14.1 m.,* revenue $9.4 m.), and wool and worsted cloths (consumption $5.7 m., revenue $3.9 m.). The taxes on manufactures of flax, hemp, cot-

* $14.1 m. = $14,100,000.

ton, iron, steel, leather, copper, lead, tin, and wood, also all enter into the cost of clothing, furniture, houses, and all other first necessaries and luxuries. The customs revenue of the United States unquestionably is paid by labor in the popular sense of that term, that is, by unskilled laborers, farmers, and mechanics.

A strong argument may be made for such taxes in a democracy. No man ought to have a share in political power unless he also bears political burdens. It is impossible to establish a sound commonwealth on any other principle. Hitherto the people of the United States have consisted to such a great majority of property holders, that the condition was practically fulfilled, although theoretical doctrines were held which recognized no such principle. With the filling up of the land, new circumstances arise. The great cities already feel the unendurable pressure of a state of things in which some people have the power without the responsibility, the rights without the duties, of citizens. They pay the taxes and bear the burdens of the national government, and they bear a great part of the local taxation, but they do not know it. Hence the education of taxation is lost upon them. Direct taxes have the advantage of bringing home to every one just what the state costs him, and the advantages both to the citizen and to the state are very great. Taxes on labor cut off the formation of capital by the laboring class, the aggregate of whose savings constitutes, both politically and economically, a fact of prime importance. It is very doubtful, therefore, whether the argument in favor of taxes on commodities in a democracy will hold good.

Local taxation takes the form generally known as direct, and it is unquestionably heavy. It is laid without system, or knowledge, by incompetent and ever-changing boards, and it forms a heavy burden on property owners, and capitalists. It is in their power to redress themselves whenever they will spend the necessary energy. They and all the rest of the people are robbed over and over again by the protective system which clings to indirect taxation. It would be a great gain to all, and in every point of view, to substitute an income tax of fifty millions for a large part of the tariff system. In favoring an income tax, however, I must be understood to do so on three conditions, under which I would favor it very earnestly, but without which I should oppose it with equal vigor. (a) It must be substituted for the customs taxes, and be used as a means of cutting off those taxes in number and amount to the greatest possible extent. To add an income tax to this cumbrous and barbarous system of duties is simply to complicate it further. We have laid a tariff averaging forty per cent. on sixteen hundred dutiable articles. It is so protective that the taxes are all paid to the protected class instead of to the government, and the revenue is inadequate. It is then proposed to make up the deficit by an income tax. (b) It must have only a very low limit of exemption. It ought to begin to operate on all incomes which are so high that they

are not fully and fairly reached by such taxes on consumption as were left. Every income tax which is
productive has to reach the great majority of incomes.
(*c*) It ought not to be progressive. Any one who
will examine the facts can assure himself that a progressive tax does not pay for the increased trouble
and cost of collecting it. A progressive tax once introduced, or even an income tax on " large incomes "
only, is a mischievous communistic arrangement.

The principle of self-taxation will have to be es-
tablished side by side with the principle of self-gov-
ernment as its necessary complement. If a man
comes forward to claim political rights, why should
he not be called forward to assume political duties?

The difficulties of " direct " taxation are that it re-
quires a good administration, and high public spirit
and morality in the people. The first is the more
important. Much stress is often laid on the disposi-
tion of people to conceal their property. This dispo-
sition, of course, exists. What is the reason for
it? The great reason is that no man in the country
has any confidence in the system of taxation. No
one believes that it is justly or efficiently administered. Each man tries to evade it because he feels
sure that his neighbors are evading it. The remedy
is to administer the system of taxation so surely,
efficiently, and exactly that this belief shall disap-
pear. If each man felt that each man was being
forced to do his full share, each would come up to his
own full share.

It is also very difficult to raise a large revenue by

direct taxation. If an income tax equal to what each one of us now pays to revenue and protection were laid on the country, it could not be collected. The tax-layer is forced to seek various and repeated modes of taxation, and to secure justice or " equality," as well as he can, by allowing these taxes to overlay each other.

I may say that I could not favor the apportionment of national taxation amongst the States per capita. It was a vicious arrangement introduced into the Federal Constitution, and cannot be modified to make it sound.

Our common enemy is protection, and I have indicated already that I am willing to co-operate in any attack on this system, or in any movement which will keep up thought and discussion about it. The question whether the government should get its revenue by direct taxes or by customs may be open for a long time yet. The question whether the government shall make A give a part of his product to B, to support B in an unproductive industry, is a question which cannot remain open long. Revenue and protection absolutely exclude each other. They have nothing in common except that they have been combined by law. The people of the United States submitted to taxation, because they thought it necessary for revenue, and the protectionists seized the opportunity to load the truly productive industries of the country with heavy burdens which give the government not one cent of revenue. Any tax which acts protectively keeps imports out. If imports are kept out they produce no revenue. Hence protection and revenue exclude each other. The tax then falls on the people, but the revenue all goes to the protected producer. In 1877 the imports of copper were $30 in value, and they paid $11.50 duty. The tax was therefore 38⅓ per cent. ad valorem, and was prohibitory, and the tax to that amount paid by the people to the American copper miners, who have the richest and most accessible mines in the world, produced not a cent of revenue. The imports of copper manufactures were $80,000, and the revenue $30,000, or 37½ per cent., which shows that the tax was almost prohibitory, but also that the tariff was a dead loss to the copper and brass manufacturers. If the copper and brass manufacturers could hold the market with less protection than the raw material had, they could hold it without any, if the raw material were free, and the system only cripples them in machinery and other supplies. If protected infants ever come of age, these two ought to be considered near it.

The question is often asked why we cannot get up a free-trade agitation here like the anti-corn-law agitation in England. Certainly no one who studies economic questions disinterestedly can help being struck again and again with the immense harm the protective system does to this country.

The case, however, is different in many respects. It is often said that England protected until she was strong and then turned to free trade. Such an assertion has not the slightest ground in historical fact. The taxes laid in Great Britain, to protect iron and wool had just as much effect as our former tax on cotton, or our present tax on breadstuffs, butter, potatoes, etc., etc., to protect agriculture. The whole truth would go further than this. The taxes referred to were injurious in many ways, as all English historians and economists agree. The free-trade agitation in England sprang from the manufacturing distress of 1836. The protected interest was agriculture, and, as one home industry cannot be protected save at the expense of another, for the simple reason that a nation cannot raise itself by taking hold of its feet any more than a man can, the protection given to agriculture in England was given at the cost of the normal and independently strong industry of the country, manufactures.

Cobden and Bright and the rest of the free-trade men got their determination from what they saw in 1836— misery, pauperism, starvation, and nakedness amongst the manufacturing laborers. They worked for ten years, spent over a half million of dollars, and then the Irish famine fairly carried them to victory. The movement was born in starvation and matured in famine.

They had two strong points for a popular movement.

1) They fought for cheap food for the people. The corn laws and provision laws kept out of England the abundance of the earth and forbade her people to eat when they were starving. The provision laws forbade the importation of butter for food, but allowed it if the butter was spoilt and only fit for

grease for machinery. To make sure that any butter imported was spoiled a custom-house officer thrust a tarred stick into it, so as to be sure of rendering it unfit for food. The protectionists have carried in their writings for a long time the story of the old Dutch East India Company destroying half the crop of spice to get a higher price for the other half than they could have got for the whole, as a specimen of commercial smartness. It is worth noticing that the Company failed; but the protectionists ought to take up the story of this custom-house officer with his tarred stick. It is a great deal better illustration of protection.

Against such laws the popular cry of "cheap food for the people" was mighty.

2) They fought against a great land-owning aristocracy. Here was another popular advantage. The English land-owners were no whit worse than the American manufacturers. I do not mean to say that the popular prejudice against a class or a section is a good or desirable weapon to use. I would not want to see it brought into our controversy, but it was a factor in the English case.

We cannot say that protection, in this country, is bringing any one to starvation. The truth in regard to protection is that *it lessens the amount of comfort and well-being of the whole people compared with what they might have had for the labor and capital expended by them.* They have less and poorer food, clothing, fuel, lights, house-room, books, education, leisure, etc., etc., than they might have had, taking the hours they labor, the capital at their disposal, and the resources of the land as they are. But the scale of comfort is so high on the average, in a new country with fresh resources, that the people do not appreciate how much better off they ought to be. A man in distress will make energetic efforts to get what he might have; a man in comfort will count the cost of securing something more, and he may submit rather than fight. Free trade will come about here by the gradual growth of the conviction that protection is all a mistake from beginning to end, for the protected, as well as for others: and then, when people go back to read the platitudes with which our contemporaries satisfy themselves about protection, they will feel the same astonishment that we do that it took past generations so long to learn religious toleration, free speech, free press, or any other development of liberty.

W. G. SUMNER.

THE TARIFF SYSTEM

AND

THE CIVIL SERVICE.

———•———

OF all the questions now pressing upon the attention of the country there is none of greater importance, none which more universally and vitally af-
fects the immediate interests of the whole people,
than that of taxation, and especially taxation by
means of a Tariff.

Nor is there any question which has so frequently
engaged the time and attention of Congress, and
been so perverted from its original purpose ; none
which has been discussed with more acrimony and
bitterness, and has produced more sectional animosity
and strife than the Tariff Revenue System.

There has been no system of public policy sustained upon such contradictory theories ; and none which
in its insidious influences has resulted in greater
injury to the manufacturing industries and the true
welfare of the country than the Tariff " Protection "
Policy.

There is nothing so full of danger to our liberties

and our cherished institutions as the continuation of
a system of revenue, capable of being so perverted
and abused.   It has developed and centralized an
enormous amount of patronage most corrupt in its
character, entirely under the control of the central
federal power and its partizans.

But at last the heavy burdens of taxation under
which the people are staggering, and the deplorable
official corruption so painfully apparent on every side,
are arousing the honest and patriotic element of the
country to demand reforms both in our Revenue
System and the Civil Service.   To accomplish results so desirable, the work must be earnestly, thoroughly and intelligently prosecuted, not by cutting
off the branches merely, but by destroying the very
roots of the system which has produced the evils from
which the country is now suffering.

BY WHOM THE BURDEN IS BORNE.

No' portion of the people have really so great an
interest in taxation and in the pure administration of
government as industrious working men and women.

Labor is the foundation on which prosperity is
based, and like the lowest stratum in any superstruc-
ture, it must necessarily bear the heaviest weight.
All taxes are a burden upon industry, and bear most
heavily upon the working classes.   They may be in
direct and hidden so that the burden is not fully com-
prehended, but it is none the less real.   The owners of
dwellings and those who are engaged in business may

be able to transfer to others some portion of their taxes by charging higher rents for their houses and higher prices for their goods, but those who are obliged to use all their earnings to meet their expenses of living, can find no one on whom to transfer any portion which directly falls upon them, and yet must bear in addition that which is shifted on them by the land-lords and traders.

No one questions the necessity for some system by which the government shall be furnished with all necessary revenue. But taxes necessarily increase the cost of living, and it is a sacred duty of Congress and of every other legislative body claiming to repre-sent the interests of the people, to adopt the simplest, most equitable and least expensive method of obtain-ing revenue; and to avoid all legislation which need-lessly increases the cost of living, or favors special interests, or which in any way interferes with industry or the natural laws of trade.

TARIFF TAXATION.

Tariff or Import Duties, although levied upon the productions of other countries, are none the less a tax which must be borne by our own people, either by paying higher prices for what we buy, or by obtaining lower prices for what we sell. This tax we cannot impose upon other countries, nor should we seek to do so. The support of our own government should appeal to our national pride, and a wholesome self-re-spect cause us to avoid any effort or desire to foist it upon others.

This import tax when levied upon articles which are not produced in this country is of comparatively limited range in its effect upon prices, while the entire amount paid by the importer goes directly into the government treasury. When, however, this tax is levied upon such articles as we do produce, and because they are produced in this country, the prices of all these articles, both domestic and foreign, are affected with this very important difference, that the increased prices of domestic goods entirely accrue to private interests, and not only afford no additional revenue to the government but actually diminish the amount it would otherwise receive. Thus when as at present, duties are levied upon every kind of goods manufactured in this country, they become a tax which increases the prices of every thing we wear ; the cost of the tools with which we work ; the rent of the houses in which we live, and even the very food that we eat. Herein lies the reason why the prices of all the necessaries of life have for years past been so enormously high, bearing with the greatest severity upon the working classes, who, notwithstanding the higher wages they receive, are obliged to pay so much more for everything they need, that they do not enjoy as many comforts as with the lower wages of the years ago, before the tariff taxes were so enormously increased. In this way their earnings are gradually but surely diverted from them, constantly tending to make them still poorer while others are enriched.

HOW MUCH THE PEOPLE PAY.

If the manufacturing interests for whose special benefit these tariff taxes have been multiplied, were required through an *excise tax* to pay to the governmen
the percentage now levied upon foreign goods, the
government, instead of the manufacturer, would receive all the difference in prices which the people pay,
and the amount added to the revenue would be sufficient to liquidate the entire National Debt within
three years. This may be shown by taking the single
item of pig-iron, which is characteristic of the entire
list. The duty on the imported iron is seven dollars
per ton in gold. Of the whole quantity used in this
country but about one-fifth is imported, and on
this the government receives revenue, while on the
other four-fifths it receives none. The price of the
entire quantity consumed, however, is increased by
the tariff. Now, if the whole were imported, or if
domestic iron paid an excise tax equal to the tariff
tax, the government treasury would receive five
times the amount now collected. And if the whole
amount of revenue from imports were thus multiplied, which would not be an excessive average if
applied to the entire list, a fair estimate can be form-
ed of the amount which the people pay through this
indirect system of taxation, without benefit to themselves or to the government.

The power to levy taxes, conferred upon Congress
by the Constitution, was intended to provide revenue
for the government, and for no other purpose. It is

2*

interesting, nay surprising, to note the advanced views
held by the convention which framed the Constitution. While leaving Congress to determine on the
method by which to provide revenue, it seemed to have
anticipated an early resort to direct taxes, and made
provision in the Constitution for the apportionment
of the amount among the States in proportion to
population and representation. One of the members
remarked in regard to the facility of this method, that
" the sum allotted to each State may be levied with-
" out difficulty according to the plan used by the
" State in raising its own supplies."

PERVERSION OF CONGRESSIONAL POWERS.

In those days, however, there was a prevailing belief in other countries, and current to a considerable
extent with our own people, that a tariff tax upon
foreign commodities conferred great benefits upon the
people by protecting their own manufacturing industries from foreign competition. Hence, in the preparation of the first tariff, it was not deemed inconsistent with the interest of the people that some
discrimination should be made in regard to certain
articles, such as cotton and woolen-goods and iron
wares, thus to be afforded to capitalists an incidental
encouragement to embark in manufacturing industries.
This was doubtless well intentioned, but under
such a form of government as ours it involved a grave
error, the magnitude of which was not realized because of the smallness of the rate, and consequently

attention was not drawn to the injurious principle on which the measure was based. It was not then seen that this was an exercise of the taxing power of Congress for the benefit of private interests, offering inducements for the investment of capital in manufacturing industries by raising an artificial barrier against foreign competition; that it was imposing a tax upon all engaged in other occupations, and who were unable or unwilling to become manufacturers. It was an adoption by the National Legislature of the *principle of special legislation*, which has since developed into such forms and proportions as to be the curse of the country. This insidious error stealthily advanced year by year in our earlier history until it gained sufficient influence and power in Congress to boldly avow and adopt PROTECTION as the policy of the government.

This policy has been persistently pursued until the original purpose of the tariff system has been completely overthrown, and instead of being a system " for revenue with incidental protection," it has become a system *for protection with incidental revenue.* Congress instead of legislating to increase the revenue of the government, now prostitutes the power delegated to it by the people to promote special interests.

AGGRANDISEMENT OF CAPITAL BY LAW.

It is this perversion and abuse of the taxing power by special legislation, aggrandizing capital, which has produced the present apparent antagonism between capital and labor ; for there is no normal antagonism between these elements of industry. No working-man finds any antagonism between his labor and the little capital he has managed to accumulate; on the contrary, he finds it a constant incentive and encouragement to him in his work. Antagonism and jealousy exist only because of the increased, un-natural, power given to the possessors of capital by laws enacted for their special benefit, without any proper consideration for the interests of the working-men—without affording them any adequate security against its abuse, and without increasing proportionately their power of self-defence.

LEGISLATION CONTROLLED BY CAPITAL.

The granting of enormous subsidies in lands to railroads, and the conferring of special privileges and immunities upon banking institutions, manufacturing corporations, and other. forms of monopoly, have given them such unnatural and overwhelming power, as to control almost the whole legislation of the country, both State and Federal, and this power, if not promptly and firmly grappled with and over thrown, will soon overpower the people themselves.

DANGER OF COUNTER LEGISLATION.

The workingmen of this country, conscious of the burden pressing upon them with increasing severity, are rapidly comprehending that the difficulty arises from the aggrandisement of capital by legislative enactments. They are steadily organizing themselves for the purpose of demanding relief from this unnatural condition of things, but there is great danger that a remedy will be sought in the enactment of new laws, rather than in the abolishment of those which have produced the injuries — which would be an attempt to correct existing evils by counter-irritants.

This course cannot be effective. It will only increase the enmity now existing between labor and capital, while there need be. no real conflict of interest, and there would be none between them if left to themselves undisturbed by legislation. Labor can always defend itself against a selfish and improper use of capital, and need ask no favor so long as both are eft equally free. Existing evils resulting from improper laws cannot be remedied by new laws to counteract those now in force, for it is equally wrong to legislate in the special interest of labor. The only way is to annul all laws which confer special advantages on either.

EXCHANGES SHOULD BE FREE.

Trade and Commerce—*i. e.*, exchanging the products of labor—are essential to the welfare of humanity. Production and exchanges are alike necessary to the prosperity and welfare of the individual and of the nation. Whether with men or with nations the same laws of trade are applicable, being limited by neither state nor national boundaries. In order to secure the largest benefits which labor and trade are capable of conferring, they should be alike libera ted from legal obstacles, and be left as free as possible to seek its highest development.

A country like ours must necessarily have extensive and important business or exchanging relations with other countries. The benefits of these exchanges are not limited to the comparatively small number of persons directly engaged in exporting or importing products and commodities, but more or less affect the interests of the whole people.

A Revenue System should at least have the merit of stability. This is equally necessary to the government, which needs steadiness of revenue, and to the people, who need steadiness in commerce and industry, and find the ordinary and unavoidable fluctuations of trade quite enough to contend with. It is not possible that frequent, irregular and arbitrary congressional changes in the revenue laws can be otherwise than injurious, in unsettling and deranging the business relations of the country. Every sensible man understands this, and if, notwithstanding, the country seems prosperous, this prosperity is not to be attributed to any tariff laws, but rather to the indomitable industry and energy of the people overcoming, in part at least, the evils of such congressional legislation.

HOW FREQUENTLY CHANGES HAVE BEEN MADE.

The Tariff System since its adoption, in 1789, has been discussed in Congress in almost every session, and has been altered or amended more than *forty* times, involving in every instance more or less

derangement of the business relations of the people.
If these derangements were of benefit to the government there might be some shadow of justification for
the action which produced them. But such legislation when enacted, as in most instances it has been,
with intent to benefit special interests—to " protect "
or "encourage" one kind of industry by taxing or
obstructing others just as legitimate, just as necessary, just as much entitled to protection, and generally more profitable to the country—is in no wise to
be justified, and is opposed to the broad and benefi-
cent principles on which our government is founded.

Mr. E. B. Bigelow, himself a Protectionist, in his
work on the tariff enumerates eighteen changes previous to 1832, viz. : in 1789, 1790, 1791, 1792, 1794, 1795,
1797, 1800, 1804, 1805, 1812, 1813, 1816, 1818, 1819,
1824, 1828, 1830, 1832. And there have been more
than twenty successive changes at irregular intervals
between 1832 and 1871.

PROTECTIONISTS NEVER SATISFIED.

The changes between 1861 and 1870 have been more
sweeping and more frequent than within any similar
period in our history. During this period the protectionists have been entirely in the ascendant, and
have without difficulty passed every measure they
desired. But they have never succeeded in satisfy-
ing even themselves. Now that they no longer have
such unlimited power, they are with cool effront-
ery appealing to the people for co-operation to

"secure stability of legislation on all questions of Tariff, Commerce and Finance!"

When so many alterations have been made in our tariff laws, averaging more than one every two years, it could not be otherwise than that the discussions relating to the subject would be increased in importance at nearly every session of Congress. With the inevitable derangement of business relations, and the clashing of the various interests of different sections of the country, these discussions have constantly increased in acrimony and bitterness, and have produced more sectional animosity and strife than that attending any other, not excepting slavery.

GRAVE QUESTIONS AS TO CONSEQUENCES.

The controversies arising from legislation on the tariff question previous to 1832, developed in that year all the elements of civil war, lacking only the strength and preparation attained in 1861, to have made it proportionately disastrous with that sad and bloody contest. Indeed it is a question whether but for the sectional strife growing out of the tariff legislation prior to 1832, there would have been a rebellion in 1861? Whether the supposed value of slave labor and its necessity to the South, did not steadily increase with the increase of protective legislation? Whether the perversion of our revenue system, in order to protect and aid manufacturing industries mainly carried on at the North, and in which the South did not desire to engage, did not more

contribute to preserve slavery, and lead to the belief
of its necessity to the people of the South than any
other cause? The change in the views of the South
regarding slavery, has been attributed by many to
the influence of the Cotton Gin; yet, as this valuable
machine was invented in 1793, and in use nearly forty
years before the advent of the nullification troubles
of 1832, is it not preposterous, nay, wicked, to charge
upon an invention capable of so great benefit to humanity, that its direct result was to intensify and
perpetuate human slavery?

PROTECTION A USURPATION OF POWER.

Protection to manufacturers is only another name
for special legislation. Manufacturing is only one
form of business, nothing more. It is just as much a
private business interest as farming or trading, or any
other form of employment. Using the power of
Congress to promote either of these interests by creat-
ing obstructions in the way of others is simply a
usurpation of power, which if persevered in, may produce another civil war as disastrous as that from
which we have so recently emerged.

HOW IT IS SUSTAINED.

The policy of protection is sustained by its advocates on widely different grounds, and for reasons
both conflicting and inconsistent. Indeed, the whole
system is founded upon contradictions and antago-
nisms, impossible to harmonize. It is inimical to the

principles of our government, and contains within itself the elements of its own destruction. Many persons honestly support it because of the supposed
benefits to the general industry of the country, while
the persistent efforts of interested, if not selfish parties,
for years past, have involved the question in so much
confusion as to prevent many from seeing that it is
entirely inconsistent with the sound principles which
men adopt in their common business affairs.

CONTRADICTIONS.

In the political conflicts growing out of it in the
various sections of the country, both advocates and
opponents of protection have been influenced by reasons and motives contradictory in principle. Protectionists so called on the one side were clamorous
for complete freedom for themselves, but persistent
in their efforts to shackle trade. Free Traders as
they were called, on the other side, were equally
strenuous in their demands for freedom in trade, while
at the same time refusing to remove the bonds from
labor. This destructive antagonism of principles has
already produced disaster on the one side. It is only
a question of time to ensure a similar result on the
other, unless averted by timely abandonment of the
whole pernicious and unnatural system.

MOTIVES FOR CONTINUING IT.

The Protective policy is advocated by a comparatively inconsiderable number of persons possessed of

large wealth, whose whole capital and whose material interests are identified with some kind of business which it is supposed derives its profits from the protective system. These have no patience with men who differ with them, and are not willing to be taxed for their supposed benefit. Having been for so long a time "encouraged" and supported by an assessment upon the industry of others, its continuance is insisted upon by the protected interests as a right. They are very fluent in declaiming about " the pauper labor of Europe," forgetting that as paupers are those who are supported at public expense by a tax upon the industry of others, this epithet may with more truthfulness be applied to themselves than to the producers of Europe.

Some defend the system from national prejudices, supposing that it can be used as a retaliatory measure towards rival countries, inflicting injuries on them, while we receive some indefinable benefit from it. It is forgotten that such measures are unworthy of a nation calling itself Christian, and through higher than human laws, must result in greater injury to those who adopt them.

Some advocate the system entirely from selfish motives, seeking to derive benefit to themselves, by imposing disadvantages upon others. It might be well for such to remember that selfishness is a mean and degrading element, one which men are instinctively reluctant to have applied to themselves, and which certainly is no less offensive and despicable as the characteristic of a nation than when found in the individual.

There are many, however, who believe that protection is necessary to the welfare of the industrious working masses of the people. Such are doubtless honest in this conviction, very intelligent on other practical subjects, but have evidently given this most important question no careful consideration. To all such it seems intricate and confusing, and they prefer to remain ignorant of its effects rather than take a little trouble to analyze it. Complaining as they do about taxes and corruption, they yet allow selfish and interested parties to control legislation, and thus continue the present evils which oppress the community.

PROTECTION DOES NOT PROTECT LABOR.

Protective legislation always has for intent to confer advantages upon capital, but neglects the interests of labor. In order to divert capital from other uses, it attempts to make it more remunerative in certain industries than in others, and is thus used professedly as a means of protecting our national industry against foreign competition. This compels the people to pay a higher price for goods, to aid certain manufacturers, and imposes a penalty on those who prefer foreign fabrics. By this policy, the people, deprived of a natural right, are obliged to pay more for clothing, tools, and other necessaries of life without being secured any increased means wherewith to pay for them. Congress has no right to require from any one a surrender of property without an equivalent, even for government purposes, yet it confers the *power* to do this upon certain manufacturers by means of the tariff. It may be that higher prices are not invariably the result, but such is nevertheless the *intention* and purpose of those who secure such legislation. It is intended to secure to certain manufacturers some advantage in the prices of the goods they produce, but does not secure or seek to secure any corresponding advantage to their workman and employès. There is not only no protection to them against the free importation of competing labor, but this is purposely left open that the manufacturers may also be protected against any demands from their workmen and employès for increased wages. Indeed, protection is demanded *expressly because wages are already so high!* It is not to furnish employment to those who are without it, but to indemnify the employers for the high rates which labor commands. These tariff assessments rest upon the whole people, including the very class who do the work of producing the protected articles.

CHANGE OF BASE.

Having succeeded in obtaining protection on the plea of high wages, having long received the supposed benefit of it, when the people think this fostering should be discontinued, an appeal is next made to the sympathies and fears of the people on the plea that if protection ceases, the workmen will be thrown out of employment, or else be obliged to work at the pauper rates prevailing in Europe.

Efforts are persistently made to produce the impression that not only the prosperity of all the working-classes, but even that of the whole country is dependent upon this protection to manufacturing industries, while the fact remains that those industries which claim to need it, are supported like paupers by a tax upon the self-sustaining industries of the country ; hence the whole country would be far more prosperous without them, if, unaided, they cannot sustain themselves.

STRIKES AND PROTECTION LAWS THE SAME.

The laws protecting manufacturers have produced the organization of Trades Unions, and the numerous Strikes which have so greatly injured labor and industry. It is through combinations of manufacturers that Congress has enacted laws whereby workingmen and all others are prevented buying goods where and from whom they please, except at artificially enhanced prices. Acting in self-defense, the workingmen combine under laws of their own making to prevent the manufacturers from employing whom they please, except on such terms and conditions as these trades unions may prescribe. Trades unions and strikes among workingmen are identical in principle with protection to manufacturers. Both attempt to secure selfish ends by compulsory means ; one seeking to obtain higher prices for their goods ; the other to secure higher prices for their labor. Both seek to accomplish their purpose by obstructing the natural laws of trade and by violating the sacred rights of individuals.

PROTECTION IN ENGLAND.

Frequent reference is made to the attempt of England during perhaps two hundred years, to build up by protection a vast system of manufactures which it is said has secured to her her present enormous accumulation of capital. We are told that when we shall have attained a similar condition, we too, like England, will be able to abandon the protective system. It is taken for granted by many, as a matter of course, that the results attained by England are attributable to the protective policy. But others are ready to dispute this. If, however, we admit that England has acquired her wealth and manufacturing pre-eminence through such a system, the question naturally arises as to which portion of her people received the benefits, the working classes, or the manufacturing capitalist? Why was it that, under a system which is claimed to be especially favorable to workingmen, the British Iron Masters and other proprietors became enormously wealthy, while the working classes were crushed and ground to the deepest degradation and poverty? Why was it that the working classes in Great Britain were so nearly starved under the protective system, that in sheer desperation they demanded and secured its repeal? And why is it that *since the repeal*, these same classes have so developed in material and intellectual and political strength, that they now influence the policy of government in matters where once they were almost entirely ignored?

PROTECTION DEFEATED BY SELF-INTEREST.

Protection so called is contrary to the laws of trade universally adopted in the management of individual affairs. Obstacles and hindrances in the way of any lawful business, are if possible removed, not interposed. When these obstacles are in the form of a statute law, efforts are made to evade its application to themselves, even by those who may have advocated its adoption. The number of men throughout the country directly interested in any one article protected is very small, while all the rest are interested in exactly the opposite direction. This is the fact in regard to each article on the list. And so almost the entire mass of the people, instinctively and persistently—perhaps unconsciously—are using every effort to neutralize the effect of protection upon every article and interest with which they are not specially identified. Here is a power, silent, but perfectly irresistible, even by law, which renders it practically impossible to secure the intended benefit of protection for any length of time, necessitating frequent alterations and additional safeguards which only serve to increase the difficulties and disarrangements which affect trade. Every business transaction is thus made more difficult and more expensive without any corresponding benefit to the great mass of the people.

DILEMMA PRESENTED BY PROTECTIONISTS.

Interested advocates of a high protective policy together with many who are deluded by their so phistries, insist upon its continuance for two very different and irreconcilable reasons.

On the one hand, an appeal is made directly to our integrity and patriotism on the ground that the nation, owing a very large debt, must have a high tariff to ensure the necessary revenue. On the other hand, our national sympathies and pride are invoked in behalf of home manufactures in order that we may not be dependent upon Europe for such fabrics as can be made here, alleging that this cannot be successfully done except under a high protective tariff.

Now here is a dilemma forced upon every one of us by these unselfish and patriotic protectionists, in which it is impossible to hold both horns at the same time. If we choose the one by which government is strengthened with revenue, then in supplying our wants we must give preference to imported fabrics, it being from these revenue is obtained. If we take the other and endeavor to encourage domestic manufactures in buying home-made goods, we may succeed in helping the manufacturers, but we thereby deprive the government of the revenue which it needs and ought to receive. The truth is, there is a direct antagonism between the interests of the government and those of the protected manufacturers. The latter nevertheless claim to be the especial friends and supporters of the government, while in reality the importers and consumers of foreign goods are its best and most reliable supporters. Those, who like some of our highest government officials, advocate the so-called American System, and boast of their higher

2

Americanism in using goods of domestic manufacture, really use their means and influence to promote some private interest, and to deprive the government of its needed revenue.

PROTECTION INJURES MANUFACTURING INDUSTRY.

The policy of protection not only tends to diminish the resources of government, but also to weaken and injure and destroy the very industries which it proposes to aid, since it undermines and destroys the *element of self-reliance* which is absolutely essential to real success in every enterprise. This is at once recognized when applied to individuals, where there is no difficulty in predicting which of any given number will be successful, those who are generously assisted by friends or those who are obliged to rely upon their own efforts. The result can be still more confidently predicted of those who are assisted by government, where no acknowledgment is required, and no return is to be made. Such assistance can only enervate and injure, hindering as it does the proper development of the spirit of self-help.

The effect of this universal principle certainly cannot be any less enervating and injurious in its results when applied to companies of men engaged in manufacturing; and the insidious but inevitable effects of the protective policy upon those industries which have always enjoyed it, are perfectly manifest in their present condition. So far from being independent and self-supporting, as they would have been if left to their own resources they are now more dependent upon this artificial support than ever before. And we are justified in the confident prediction that they *never* will become self-sustaining until left to rely upon themselves rather than on legislative assistance. To confirm this view we need but compare the present with the past. In our infancy as a nation, eighty years ago, in order to encourage these industries a duty of *five per cent.* was imposed upon cotton and woolen goods, and *seven and one-half per cent.* upon iron wares. At present *not less than ten times* this amount of security is demanded as being necessary to the very existence of these industries. More than one hundred years ago we made and exported pig iron to England, and that country thought herself compelled to protect her iron interests by forbidding its importation from the colonies. Even when our first tariff was adopted, it was not deemed necessary to include pig iron in the list. Since then (in 1815) the Protectionists attempted to make this article more profitable to its producers by a tariff tax, but this has so weakened this important and once self-sustaining trade, or has so stimulated a principle of avarice as to lead those engaged in it to claim that it cannot exist except by a subsidy of seven dollars per ton in gold, levied upon those who consume iron. So much for interests which are fostered and propped up by protection. On the other hand, in manufactures, such as sewing machines, watches, agricultural implements, and many other things peculiarly American, which require the highest degree of skill in the application of tools specially adapted to the work, and in regard to which for special reasons protection cannot operate effectively, we are taking the lead of the world, and have no fear of competition from any quarter. This success, however, is attributed by our leading protectionist organ, in a particular reference to watch-making, not to skill in manufacturing but to skillful and judicious *advertising!*

INJURIOUS EFFECTS ON AGRICULTURE.

While a long series of Congressional obstructions and hindrances has increased the price of all manufactured goods, the effect upon our staple agricultural productions has been in the contrary direction. The selfish legislation which has enhanced the cost of all we make, has compelled manufacturers in other countries to exercise more skill and greater economy —to develop the self-reliant element—and thus they are still able to send their wares here, besides completely shutting us out from the markets which we once almost controlled. Our agricultural products are increasing much more rapidly than a home market can possibly be made for them by any system of legislation. A market for the surplus has thus become not only essential, but it is quite as important that those who desire this surplus shall be in a thriving condition, and thus enabled to pay us fair prices for it. The prices obtained abroad for our surplus products materially affect the value of our whole production, and thus the English market regulates our prices at home. Everywhere throughout the country, where the farmer sells his grain, the buyer is governed by the New York quotations, and these in turn by those of London. Thus the effect of our protective policy is to increase the cost of goods made here, and to diminish the cost of making goods in the country where we sell our surplus. It increases the cost of what we buy, and reduces the price of what we sell. We deprecate the low rates of wages and consequent poverty among the working classes in Europe, yet pursue a policy which depresses their condition still more, and lessens their ability to buy and consume what we are compelled to sell there.

ASSUMED BENEFITS OF PROTECTION.

Exultant protectionists sometimes point to places in this country which have been entirely built up by manufactures, as an evidence of the wealth and prosperity produced by those industries. They are careful, however, never to mention the fact that they are not self-sustaining; but that by taxing the whole people through the tariff system, this wealth is drawn there from other places and concentrated in these fewer hands, and that hard-working people far away who cannot derive any possible benefit from this transfer and concentration of wealth, are obliged through this vaunted American System to pay higher prices for what they buy, to enrich the places where these manufactures flourish.

If these forced contributions were only levied on those who derive benefits and profits from these manufacturing establishments; from those whose proper-

ty is increased in value, and who receive the benefits
of this home market—if these alone were compelled to
bear the whole expense of the system, there would
soon be a change in their estimate of the value of
protection to domestic industries in order to create
home markets. They would soon adopt the very in-
elegant, but forcible language used by the foremost
newspaper advocate of protection in this country, in
reply to the poor freedmen of the South who asked
the government to aid (protect?) them a little longer,
" Root, Hog or Die ! "

CENTRALIZED POWER IN THE REVENUE SYSTEM.

The Tariff System has been so thoroughly perverted from its original purpose that it now mainly
promotes private interests positively antagonistic to
those of the government, and its administration has
become fearfully corrupt. By means of it the federal
patronage has grown to enormous and dangerous proportions, and it will continue to grow as the country
grows, while the system is continued. When to this is
added that other most formidable power, our Internal
Revenue System, equally corrupt with the Tariff, the
patronage in the control of the government becomes
an almost overpowering means of acquiring and re-
taining political power by corrupt and unscrupulous
men. These systems require the services of many
thousand men and an expenditure of many millions
of dollars. Besides the "ins" who hold offices there
is a still greater number of "outs" who want their
places, and the most unscrupulous means are used to

nold or to obtain official position. The men who live
by politics are incessantly engaged in manœuvring the
political parties to which they respectively belong.
These "ins" and "outs" between them, control all
the nominations for office as well as all the elections.
It matters not which party is in the ascendant, this is
the class of men who secure party success, and must
therefore be rewarded in the distribution of the federal patronage. To control and dispense this patronage
is, more than anything else, that for which parties contend. The existence of such a gigantic, overshadowing, centralized power, was never contemplated by
the founders of our government, and no party ought
to be entrusted with it. It is the most dangerous element with which the people have to contend, and
their energies cannot too earnestly or too promptly
be directed to its overthrow. Any proposed reform
in our national affairs, which does not seek to remove
entirely this vast element of corruption, cannot be
successful.

WHY THE TARIFF SYSTEM WAS CHOSEN.

In the crude and unsettled condition of public affairs, when Congress first acted on the question of
revenue, under the power conferred by the Constitution, instead of adopting the method of direct taxation
by apportionment among the States therein provided
for, the system of Import Duties was unfortunately
determined on. This may have arisen from the well-
known jealousy on the part of the States, lest too

much power should be exercised by the general gov ernment. Yet doubts seem to have existed whether a Tariff System would work satisfactorily, since the first tariff was limited to a period of seven years duration. It was made a definite policy for this specified time, probably to create a basis of national credit to facilitate the negotiation of the loans needed by the Treasury, as European countries then had more confidence in such methods of revenue than in any other.

If the system of direct taxation by apportionment among the States had then been adopted, the collections would have been made through the ordinary agencies of the several States, each in its own way. The corrupt Custom House machinery would not have been developed. Congress would have been kept from sectional legislation, and the country would no doubt have been spared the sad sectional strife which has lately destroyed so much useful wealth and so many valuable lives.

OBJECTIONS TO APPORTIONMENT ANSWERED.

There are not wanting, those who contend that the States, under an apportionment system will not respond to their allotted quota, some of them having once, before the Constitution was adopted, refused to do so. But who can believe that the people who have so recently and thoroughly proved their faithfulness by submitting to every form of taxation almost at the same time, will ever again permit their respective

States to refuse their just quota to the national expenditures? Looking at the enormous burdens of taxation quadrupled through the tariff, and the deplorable official corruption created by that system, who can doubt that the people would now prefer to go back to where our fathers once stood and make a new and sounder beginning in our Revenue System?

If, when our revenue system was first adopted it could have been foreseen what incalculable evils would grow out of the tariff—from the perversion of its purpose and the abuse of its power, from the sectional strife, the official corruption, and the dangerous federal patronage it created—who can doubt that in those days of at least comparative purity, Congress would have overwhelmingly adopted a system of direct taxation as the national policy?

Had it been foreseen that the effect of encouraging manufactures through the tariff taxation would only enervate the men engaged in them, and make them increasingly dependent—that after eighty years of artificial fostering, these industries would require ten times additional stimulus to keep them alive; who can doubt that these industries would have been left, as individuals are left, to their own self-reliant energy and to their individual self-interest, *which is the* ONLY TRULY AMERICAN SYSTEM, *the only true method of developing manufacturing or any other form of industry?*

The simple system of unrestricted freedom in trade and commerce, is the natural and right condition, and the *only* system in harmony with the principles of our government. Barriers are the work of governments and should never be interposed except from absolute necessity—never with the purpose to benefit ourselves by placing others at a disadvantage. Individuals and corporations too often resort to such measures, but this should be considered unworthy of a great government. Even if a tariff could be framed that would secure sufficient revenue from articles which we do not produce, the rate must not only be very high but the temptation to fraud and adulteration in quality of goods would be greatly increased. This, for several years, has been carried on to such an extent in the article of coffee, by some counted one of the necessaries of life, that it has been almost impossible to obtain it pure, and the same experience is now threatened in regard to tea. If adulteration should not always result, still the price must be so much enhanced as to diminish the consumption, and thus injure our exchanging relations with the countries producing these articles. We may add to this, that any such business will necessarily require so much more capital to conduct it, that it becomes practically a monopoly controlled by a few men.

WHAT MIGHT HAVE BEEN.

A thoroughly ANTI-PROTECTIVE policy from the first, thoroughly persevered in, might have prevented much of the legislative favoritism, much of the vast federal patronage and the corruption with which the country is cursed ; but so many phases of special legislation have been developed and endorsed

by the usages under the tariff system, that no effective remedy can now be secured, except by entirely
abolishing our present method, and adopting one
which will be uniform and permanent. Besides, a
tariff purely anti-protective will not produce sufficient revenue for an economical administration of
government, so that some internal revenue system
must also be necessary. This will require the continuance of all the machinery now in use, with most
of its attendant corruption, extravagance, and other
evils; and these means of securing a centralising
power every political party will seek to perpetuate.

WILL THE PEOPLE OPPOSE DIRECT TAXATION?

Many insist that the people at large are opposed to
direct taxation, and even prefer to pay a much larger
amount indirectly. This is simply equivalent to
asserting that the people, at heart, are unfaithful to
our institutions, and must be *cheated* into supporting
them, or else they are so stupid that, like children,
they must be hoodwinked into it. This cannot be
true of the people. It is only the pretence of those
who misrepresent them and desire that a corrupt
and extravagant system of legislation be continued,
for their own selfish ends. Taxation has, indeed, become odious to the people, and may yet drive them
to repudiation; but it has been made odious by the
multitude of indirect methods resorted to in order
to filch an excessive amount to be used for nefarious
and corrupt purposes. The people will readily pay

for supporting a purely administered government,
when confined to its legitimate sphere, and so long
as those who are entrusted with power are faithful
to their trust and loyal to the people, whose ser-
vants only they are. The people will meet promptly
and honestly all proper obligations, if those who
exercise legislative powers will deal honestly with
them. But they may be educated to dishonesty and
repudiation by the continuation, and that only for a
few years longer, of the excessive and indirect and
multitudinous forms of taxation now in operation.

Some will be ready to urge, in order to avoid any
change, that the basis of taxation, through State apportionment, according to representation and population, is unequal and unfair; that some States may
thus be required to pay too large a proportion,
which they will not submit to. It must be remem-
bered that the principles of our national government
are not based upon property but *upon men*, and its
functions should be exercised alike in the interest of
all. From this view of the question, after a most
thorough discussion of it, the framers of the Constitution unanimously decided in favor of the principle
of direct taxation in proportion to population and representation, as being equitable and just. Property representation, in other relations, may be right, but not so
in the general government, in which every man has
a right to an equal interest and voice. Besides, if
the apportionment system is any better than the
present system, if it materially reduces taxes, as
it must, the change will be for the nation a great

stride in the right direction, while the question of local taxation will be open all the more readily to any modification or improvement which experience can suggest.

The radical change which we propose may find objectors, from an undue apprehension of disasters resulting from an immediate or sudden remodeling of our system, but it cannot be sudden or immediate, inasmuch as there is time required to educate the people, and then to secure action through Congress, and this will afford ample notice to all the interests to be affected.

APPORTIONMENT ILLUSTRATED.

Let us illustrate more definitely the practical working of an apportionment system, showing also how largely the burdens of taxation for supporting the government would fall on the wealthier States, while the proportion of each State would be much less than it is under the present system.

The following statement has been carefully condensed from the government statistics; the revenue returns being for the year 1875, and the population from the census of 1870:

Am't of Revenue from Import Duties	$157,167,722.35	
" " " Internal Excise	110,007,493.58	
		$267,175,215.93
Less for Refundings, Drawbacks, Debentures, etc...............		5,311,602.84
Net Receipts....................... ..		261,863,613.09
Deduct for cost of collecting Salaries,etc.,		
Import..	7,926,507.65	
Internal.	4,289,442.71	
		12,215,950.36
Net Revenue, less cost of collecting................$249,647,662.73		

Here is a net total from these two sources of $249,647,662.73, costing the people the additional sum of $12,215,950.36 in salaries and similar expenses, and employing over twenty thousand office-holders, who seem to think it a large part of their duty to manage the machinery of politics. This is without saying anything about the erection and maintenance of buildings at the four hundred and ninety customs stations, or of other expenditures not included in the table, the addition of which would greatly augment this exhibit.

The net sum which was realized by the government amounts to a little less than $6.50 per capita on the census of 1870, when the population was 38,558,371 —on this number a per capita tax of $6.50 would amount to $250,629,411. If it were divided among the States pro rata to be collected, and thereby a saving of more than twelve millions of dollars effected, the portion falling upon each State would be as follows :

	STATES AND TERRITORIES.	Population 1870.	State Tax by Apportionment at $6.50 per capita.
1	New York	4,382,759	$28,487,933.50
2	Pennsylvania	3,521,951	22,892,681.50
3	Ohio	2,665,260	17,324,190.00
4	Illinois	2,539,891	16,509,291.50
5	Missouri	1,721,295	11,188,417.50
6	Indiana	1,680 637	10,924,140.50
7	Massachusetts	1,457,351	9,472,781.50
8	Kentucky	1,321,011	8,586,571.50
9	Tennessee	1,258,520	8,180,380.00
10	Virginia	1,225,163	7,963,559.50
11	Iowa	1,194,020	7,761,130.00
12	Georgia	1,184,109	7,696,708.50
13	Michigan	1,184,059	7,696,383.50
14	North Carolina	1,071,361	6,963,846.50
15	Wisconsin	1,054,670	6,855,355.00
16	Alabama	996,992	6,480,448.00

STATES AND TERRITORIES.	Population 1870.	State Tax by Apportionment at $6.50 per capita.
17 New Jersey....	906,096	$5,889 624.00
18 Mississippi......................	827,922	5,381,493.00
19 Texas....	818,579	5,320,763.50
20 Maryland......	780,894	5,075,811.00
21 Louisiana...........	726,915	4,724,947.50
22 South Carolina............	705,606	4,586,439.00
23 Maine....................	626,915	4,074,947.50
24 California..................	560,247	3,641,605.50
25 Connecticut................	537,454	3,493,451.00
26 Arkansas.......	484,471	3,149,061.50
27 West Virginia..............	442,014	2,873,091.00
28 Minnesota..........	439,706	2,858,089.00
29 Kansas.....................	364,399	2,368,593.50
30 Vermont..................	330,551	2,148,581.50
31 New Hampshire............	318,300	2,068,950.00
32 Rhode Island..............	217,353	1,412,794.50
33 Florida..................	187,748	1,220,362.00
34 Delaware.................	125,015	812,597.50
35 Nebraska.................	122,993	799,454.50
36 Oregon...................	90,923	590,999.50
37 Nevada...................	42,491	276,191.50
1 District of Columbia..............	131,700	856,050.00
2 New Mexico.................	91,874	597,181.00
3 Utah......................	86,786	564,109.00
4 Colorado..................	39,864	259,116.00
5 Washington...............	23,955	155,707.50
6 Montana..................	20,595	133,867.50
7 Idaho....................	14,999	97,493.50
8 Dakota...................	14,181	92,176.50
9 Arizona..................	9,658	62,777.00
10 Wyoming.................	9,118	59,267.00
	38,558,371	$250,629,411.50

The statement made up on the census of 1870 showing that $6.50 per capita would have been more than
sufficient in 1875, it is safe to calculate that, on the
census of 1880, the population will have increased
enough to reduce the per capita to five dollars. This

for an average family of six persons would be thirty
dollars a year. Now where is there a family which,
under the present system, is not subjected to a
much larger sum than this? There is scarcely an
article of food or clothing, or tools or farming implements that the mechanic or farmer buys that is
not increased in price at least forty per cent. through
the tariff.

That is, on every hundred dollars' worth which he
buys, at least forty dollars of it is a tax, added because of the tariff. There is not an article of manufactured goods of any kind that is free from this tax;
the lumber in a house, the paint, the glass, the nails, the
screws, the furniture,—everything is taxed, and this
too, not so much for the government as for those who
make these things. It bears with peculiar severity
upon the farmer, for he is obliged to sell his farm products at foreign prices and buy his supplies on the
tariff-increased prices of the home market.

The amount of the so-called per capita tax would
not be levied on and collected from every family or
individual directly, but would be added to and included in the amount which the State apportions to,
and collects from, the counties in the ordinary way.
Of course the annual tax bills would be increased, but
the annual expenses of the family would be reduced
more than enough to pay the difference.

This statement only shows a beginning of results
which may be expected to flow from a dividing of the
amount among the States, to be collected by them.
The economy and simplicity should alone be suffi-

cient to recommend it, the government would be released from those heavy expenses which the complicated machinery of customs and excise make necessary, and the National Treasury would receive clean sums in bulk from the State Treasurers. There would be no additional cost to the States for collecting, as all the machinery exists and is paid for by the States, to officials who are not appointed by the government, but are chosen by the people themselves. This would be a strong check upon the centralizing tendency of the general government, and would remove from national politics a very large body of office-holders numbered by thousands connected with the Import and Internal Revenue Service. What this means it is scarcely necessary to suggest to any intelligent citizen. It would not only reform the Civil Service by abolishing these offices, but remove from the political arena the number of office-holders more than four times multiplied, of those who, in both parties, are anxious to get these places as rewards for party service, and are not over-scrupulous in the means used to accomplish their object.

THE PEOPLE DEMAND REFORM.

The oppressive burdens of taxation and the widespreading official corruption are arousing the people to demand reform in both the Revenue System and the Civil Service. But how is it possible to secure these reforms so absolutely necessary, while the present systems are continued in operation? The tariff has never been exempt from the tampering officiousness of Congress, and never will be so long as special legislation can be purchased. The Civil Service can never be reformed while there are so many offices to be filled, and so many ready to use corrupt means to obtain these offices, with full purpose to make them remunerative, no matter at what expense they may have been secured. All the interests of corrupt office-holders, and all the ambition of office-seekers in Congress and elsewhere, are thus directly arrayed against these reforms, which can only be accomplished by the people making a bold, determined, uncompromising effort to secure a thorough change in our whole revenue system. In this way only can thousands of offices be abolished, millions of dollars now spent in salaries be saved, and a very large proportion of the corrupt and dangerous element now overshadowing the country be destroyed.

WHO WILL OPPOSE REFORM.

The honest and patriotic men of the country demand these reforms,—men who are not ambitious for office, and who prefer the welfare of the country above party success. There is a majority of such in each of the existing parties, but their power is entirely annulled by the skill of the leaders. A movement in the right direction is sure to draw this element to its support. Protectionists, who wish to thrive by a tax on other interests; ambitious men who are ready to use almost any means which will secure to themselves official prominence; office-

holders and office-seekers who wish to live and fat-
ten on corruption, cannot be expected to show any
favor to such a movement. They will probably
attack it covertly and openly in every way to prevent its success. But all who really desire a reduc-
tion of taxes and other public burdens; all who desire an economical and honestly administered government; all who desire reform in our civil service;
all who are true friends to domestic manufactures,
developed and sustained through self-reliant energy,
are sure to give their earnest support to such a
movement.

ORIGINAL FREE TRADERS.

There are many persons scattered through the
country, who have *always* held that " Free Trade and
Direct Taxation," is the true national policy for our
government, believing it not only far more economical and far less corrupting than any tariff system,
but also more in harmony with the principles on
which our government is founded. These especially
can be relied on for united aid and support. Never
before has there been such a combination of circumstances calling for the promulgation of true and
sound principles with so promising a prospect of
hearty response from the people, and such hopeful
assurances of success.

There are many thousands of the people who believe in the universal brotherhood of man; who
profess to believe in the doctrine of dealing with
others as they themselves would be dealt with; who

acknowledge the obligation to "preach the gospel to every creature" by sending abroad the missionary of the Cross; who believe in a time coming when righteousness and peace shall prevail in all the earth. It is certain that the breaking away of all selfish barriers between the nations, must precede the incoming of that day. Then surely the appeal which we make to the *Christian* men of the land, for coöperation in harmony with their faith, will not be unheeded? Is it not a work in which America should take the lead? We have been held up as an example to the world in every struggle for freedom. Claiming to have secured freedom of soil, freedom of speech, freedom of labor, freedom of men; to be completely consistent with our principles, we must secure like freedom in exchanging the products of labor, which is the necessary complement of the others. Let us, so far as we are able, emancipate trade and commerce from every shackle, and throw down the gauntlet of unfettered competition to all the world.

BENEFI-CENCE AND COMMON SENSE IN TRADE.

Comfort and wealth and civilization are the direct result of exchanging the surplus productions of labor between individuals and States and nations. Farmers or mechanics or artisans do not promote their comfort or wealth or knowledge by keeping all that they have themselves produced or acquired, but by using their surplus as a purchasing power to obtain something else which others have produced.

It is therefore essential to liberty and progress that men should be free to exchange productions—to sell and to buy—in any market which they or their agents

can reach; and to do it with the greatest possible·
facility, without interference by the government.

This is a degree of freedom, which, with all our
boasted liberty, the people of this country have not
yet attained. We are entitled to it, and do not think
it *necessarily* a difficult work to accomplish. " Where
there is a will there is a way." *There is a way; we
need only the will.*

Let common sense take the place of old prejudices.
Adopt in national affairs the same methods of doing
business as are universally practiced in individual
transactions. Make provision for supporting the national government as for other necessary expenses
in State or county, so that all may understand what it
costs. It is not creditable to any man that he pre-
fers to be ignorant of his family or business expenses;
why should he be willing to be deluded or hoodwinked
in regard to his portion of national expenses? Igno-
rance or blindness certainly will not make them less.
The fearful burdens of taxation, the profligacy, the
extravagance, the enormous amount of national, State
and county debts for which every house and farm in
the country is heavily mortgaged, is traceable directly
to this prolific source of evils. Let the government
expenses be paid in a way more worthy of a free people, and not by special legislation, which greatly increases the cost of living, and makes it impossible to
know how *much* the people pay, and how *little* of it
reaches the national treasury.

Other nations, where the people have never been
taught otherwise than to allow the government to

interfere with and attempt to regulate business matters; where they do not understand that government cannot possibly help some without doing corresponding injury to others;—other nations, we say, may be very far from allowing this individual or commercial freedom, but the earnest and cordial responses we are receiving from all parts of the country point unmistakably to the conclusion that our people are awaking from their dreamy indifference, and that the time is close at hand when their intelligent common-sense will grapple with this difficulty, and break at once and forever the shackles with which prejudice and selfish legislation have confined and oppressed the agricultural and other enriching industries of the nation.

Our industries need and must have freedom in using the markets of the world in which to sell and to buy. If other nations will not reciprocate by removing the barriers which they have erected, *we can overcome at least one-half the obstacles by removing those which we have put in the way.*

This is not a party question. Existing political parties have not the moral quality or courage to do anything which threatens to reduce the office-holding patronage of the government—on this, more than anything else, do they rely for success. It is for the people to strike at the very root of party corruption by abolishing a multitude of needless offices and dismissing an army of expensive, meddling office-holders, and consent to support the government in a more simple, direct and economical manner.

The present is a peculiarly appropriate time for inaugurating such a movement. Nations are being drawn closer together. Steam and electricity are almost annihilating space and time. Other barriers are rapidly disappearing. The signs of the times all point in this direction. The triumph of peace in the recent treaty between England and America foreshadows the extinction of national jealousies. What nobler object can be presented to those who wish to promote the highest welfare of the country and of the world? This work will be accomplished sooner or later, and some one country must begin it. Nothing can be more worthy the fame of America and her position among the nations, than to take the lead in a movement, which more than any other, will promote peace and good-will among the nations of the world.

COMMENDATORY.

WM. LLOYD GARRISON, *in* 1868.

NATIONAL selfishness is as much more to be deprecated than personal greed, as aggregated millions are of more consequence than the individual. Who shall rightfully interpose barriers to the unobstructed interchange of the results of human industry, invention and skill? Assuming that the interests of all nations are the interests of each, and each of all, I know not where the lines are to be drawn. If Japan and China are getting sufficiently enlightened to abandon their exclusiveness as against commercial interchange with the rest of mankind, surely the United States should take the lead in the adoption of a Free Trade policy, which, while founded upon world-wide considerations, cannot fail to be twice blessed—"blessing him who gives and him who takes," in the spirit of mutual reciprocity and good will,

HENRY WARD BEECHER, *in* "*The Christian Union.*"

FREEDOM is the breath of all true prosperity. Freedom in politics makes strong states. Freedom in religion produces pure and intelligent churches. Freedom of trade makes a sound commerce. Freedom of labor—freedom of the individual to emigrate, to choose his own market, to make his own bargains, to augment his own wages by augmenting the value of his own labor—is indispensable to the permanent prosperity of the great community of working men.

COMMENDATORY.

From "A RUN THROUGH EUROPE," *by* E. C. BENEDICT.

THE robbers of the Rhine are dead, and their castles are in ruins, and we are sailing down between their graves. The robbers of the Rhine! How easy it is to call names! They only levied duties on the commerce that passed that way; their castles were custom-houses. There were thirty-two of them in the middle ages. They were collectors, and had their night inspectors, and tide waiters, and revenue cutters, which they wore at their sides in a scabbard; their duties were *ad-valorem*, or specific by a sliding scale, always sliding upward, or in any direction in which they would produce the most revenue ; *theirs was strictly a revenue tariff.* THEY WERE ROBBERS; what are we who seize by the throat figuratively every merchant that brings us what we want, and will not let his goods pass till he has paid us a tribute of often one-third their value.

GERRIT SMITH, 1867.

WITH the high tariff men I am for promoting "American industry;" and with them I am for bringing the producer and consumer as near together as practicable. Nevertheless, I am an absolute free-trader. I would have no custom-house on the face of the earth. Never will government be administered honestly and frugally until the cost of administering it is paid by direct taxation. And never will government be confined within its proper limits until its sole office shall be to protect persons and property.

LETTER FROM REV. T. S. HASTINGS, D. D.

NEW YORK, *March* 19, 1872.

MR. A. L. EARLE.

My Dear Friend:—I have read your tract on "Free Trade" with care and with much interest. It has converted me. Educated a protectionist, politically and socially, I have been gradually losing confidence in my old convictions, as found them conflicting with those broad moral views of the oneness of humanity which the Gospel inculcates; and now your tract has broken the last tie that held me to my early opinions.

I am most happy to acknowledge myself as having become a "free trader" by the tuition of one of my earliest, best and truest friends.

Of course I think your statements clear, strong and convincing, and cheerfully commend them to the earnest attention of others. Very cordially yours,

THOMAS S. HASTINGS.

LETTER FROM CHARLES A. GURLEY, ESQ.

PULASKI, N. Y., *May 2d*, 1872.

DEAR SIR:—The pamphlet so ably advocating *Free Trade*, is clear, logical, sound, and must commend itself, in all its main features, to every unprejudiced patriot throughout our common country. Its aim is simply even-handed justice to *all* in substitution for a system that works evil continually, protecting the few at the expense of the many.

All unjust statutes, whether State or National, legitimately weaken the respect for a government, originating the sowing seeds of *Communism, riot and disorder.*

So long as machinery for raising money out of the savings of the people can be both unseen and effective, so long will lavish and unnecessary appropriations be made, and no cure so effectual, I apprehend, can be found as to have the States collect each its share of taxes. This will strengthen the interest in, and watchfulness over the perpetuity of our government. Respectfully yours,

CHARLES A. GURLEY.

ABM. L. EARLE, ESQ., New York.

From N. Y. EVENING POST, *March* 25, 1872.

Free trade is only one of the many forms of unrestrict·
ed human action which poets, philosophers and the common
people worship under the name of liberty, and, like freedom
of thought, freedom of speech, freedom of association, freedom of religious observance, is an imprescriptible right of
man; which guaranties his manhood and assures the num-
berless blessings of a high and beneficient civilization.

Free trade but expresses the world-old and universal prac-
tice of all rational beings when it asserts—which is all it asserts—that it is better for men to procure the commodities
they need by exchange than by production, when the exchange is cheaper than the production. Go into our fields,
our workshops, our mills, our stores, our shipping-houses, and
every practical man there will tell you that he would be a
fool who would waste ten hours' labor in producing for himself what he might get from another in exchange for six
hours' labor. Every individual of our forty millions of people, in his relations with other individuals, acts upon this
principle; every family in our ten millions of families, in its
relation to other families, acts upon this principle; every
township of our many thousand townships, in its relation to
other townships, acts upon this principle; every state of our
thirty-eight states and nine territories, in its relation to
other states and territories, acts upon this principle; and yet
the principle is pronounced a heresy, and the application of
it to that larger agglomeration of men called the nation is re
sisted as if it were something new, unprecedented, dangerous
and awful! What the individuals of every civilized country
all do, what the families of every civilized society all do, what
the towns and cities and states and provinces of every civilized society all do, nations may not do, as if nations were
more mysterious and inscrutable entities, differing from
every other aggregate of men.